How Students Have Changed

A Call To Action For Our Children's Future

By Julia Stratton

Preface

For the first time in history, a generation of young people is expected to fare worse economically than their parents. We are afraid for them — afraid they'll never live the American dream. At the same time, we don't always understand them, and that makes it difficult to help them achieve that dream.

Who are the students of today? What motivates them, worries them, distracts them, angers them, thrills them?

Today's students seem different because they are different. Their world is far removed from what ours was in decades past, and has affected them in both positive and negative ways. To understand today's students, we need to understand that their behavior, their attitudes and feelings, their activities and lifestyles stem from their unique values and culture.

This is a booklet about change — change among our nation's students and change within society itself. It was written not only for educators, but also for parents, business, community, and government leaders.

As part of the 1994 National Superintendent of the Year Program, cosponsored by the American Association of School Administrators and the ServiceMaster Company, finalists from all 50 states received questionnaires asking them to identify 10 major ways students had changed since the 1960s. They also shared their views and insights on how best to deal with the challenges facing today's students, educators, and communities because of those changes. Their responses, combined with the views of the teachers and others who observe our nation's children and youth, formed the backdrop for this book.

The Introduction provides a snapshot of contemporary culture and a brief overview of how past decades shaped America today. Part I lists the 10 major changes our school leaders found characteristic of today's students. Part II, which is divided into five sections, examines these changes in depth, and Part III includes recommendations from top educators for addressing these changes.

(continued on the next page...)

We encourage educators, parents, and communities to use this one-of-a-kind publication to build an even better understanding of our nation's children and youth and to spur discussions about how we can help them live even fuller, more productive lives tomorrow.

—Paul D. Houston
Executive Director
American Association of School Administrators

Introduction:

Putting Today In Context

"I don't find all this `looking back' to the past surprising. It's just part of a well-regulated society — you're always trying to define where you're going by where you've been. In a future-oriented society like ours, it's a means of projecting the old days onto the new, so we can somehow fuse the two and create a controlled and familiar universe."

—C. Duncan Rice, dean, Faculty Arts & Science, New York University
Faith Popcorn, The Popcorn Report, *Doubleday, 1991, p. 242*

Since the dawn of man, adults have decried the young, for the young, after all, represent change — change in values, attitudes, beliefs, interests, and lifestyles. While many of us might yearn for yesterday, those days are long gone.

To fully comprehend the depth and scope of the changes our leading educators observed among today's students, we must understand the sociocultural context and trends that gave birth to these changes. Hence, we begin our cultural journey with the '50s, the era in which the baby boomers were reared.

The '50s: Green Lawns, the McCarthy Hearings, Miss Clairol, and Wonderbread

During the 1950s patriotism was high and family, community, and worship held special meaning for Americans. The vast majority of children grew up with both of their natural parents. Gender roles were largely unchallenged and most mothers stayed at home to care for their families. Children participated in activities that reinforced the values of home, school, and church, such as the Boy and Girl Scouts. But even then, the seeds of change were being sown...

TV hypnosis. The TV generation tuned in. Families abandoned the dining room table for the TV tray. Edward R. Murrow warned ominously, "If television and radio are to be used for the entertainment of all of the people all of the time, we have come perilously close to discovering the real opiate of the people."

On radio, on "American Bandstand," and on "The Ed Sullivan Show," rock 'n' roll rocked American culture itself. Girls in bobby socks and saddle shoes swooned to Fabian, Bobby Vinton, the Everly Brothers, and Elvis Presley. The new music reflected a new breed of teenagers that would later become rebels with a cause.

"If we lose our sense of history — our reference point — we'll lose what we want to preserve. In short, we'll acclimate to what reality is now. We've lost our sense of values."

—Barbara Johnson, school counselor and former teacher for 20 years, Bertha Reid Elementary, Thornton, Colorado

The rumblings of change. While in retrospect the 1950s seemed an era of remarkable stability, prosperity, homogeneity, values cohesion, and hope, this decade also was a period of transition in values, in lifestyles, and in the marketplace. Landmark events such as the 1954 Brown vs. Board of Education Supreme Court decision that ended legalized segregation, the Sputnik space exploration, and the McCarthy hearings, spurred a feeling of restlessness and individualism that sent shock waves throughout American life and youth.

The '60s: The Times They Are A-Changin'

Moral relativism and contradiction were the zeitgeist of the '60s. Despite the fact that less than 20 percent of Americans actually demonstrated or rioted, this decade was much more chaotic than its predecessor. Family and community, work and team ethics, respect for authority, and respectability appeared to give way to self-expression manifested in Beatlemania, Woodstock, mantras and astrology, faded and torn blue jeans, long hair, free love, non-violence, violence, and drugs. And, we watched it all — together — on television — as the media magnified the reality.

The '60s were the years of experimentation and protest: black militarism, Vietnam protesters, the glorification of single life, and sexual freedom. In contrast to their parents who were seen and not heard, the youthful voices of challenge were broadcast throughout the land.

Something Happened in the '70s

In the wake of the Kennedy and Martin Luther King assassinations in the '60s, America's innocence continued to fade. The energy crisis and inflation; the spiralling divorce rate; the Equal Rights Amendment and feminism; and Watergate intensified the sociocultural values tug-of-war between young and old characteristic of the '60s.

The first living room war, Vietnam — and the first war America had ever lost — epitomized America's outlook. Not surprisingly, psychotherapy and self-help books flooded the shelves. As Morris Massey wrote in *The People Puzzle* (1979), "The proliferating flock of teachers, doctors, psychologists, counselors, social workers, and juvenile court officers . . . assumed the family's main function: raising children."

The '80s: Dynasty, Food Processors, and Yuppies

The early 1980s ushered in the era of the yuppie and getting rich quick during a period of relative affluence, which gave many young people a false sense of financial security. But these feel-good years were short-lived. Few were prepared for the devastating recession of the late '80s. The savings and loan crisis foreshadowed many scandals to come. In fact, the good life, anchored in hope, faded into uncertainty, mistrust, and cynicism.

The Numbing '90s

As "Generation X" grows up witnessing the videotaped Rodney King beating and subsequent Los Angeles riots, Clarence Thomas-Anita Hill hearings, abortion clinic killings, the O.J. case, and the bombing of the Alfred P. Murrah Building in Oklahoma City; some would argue young people have lost not only their boundaries of right and wrong, but also their hope and faith in a better tomorrow.

At the same time, students are ecologically and globally aware as never before. The popular music-video channel, MTV, urges teenagers to vote and to end racism and prejudice (though ironically, many of its videos depict the negative practices it protests). Many young people seek meaning in their lives through volunteering, church causes, or peer counseling. For most, idealism survives despite the odds.

In this context, then, we turn to our list of the top 10 changes school leaders believe characterize our young people on the eve of a new century.

Part One:

On The Charts!

The Top 10 Changes Among Our Students Since the 1960s

The 1994 Superintendent of the Year state finalists were surveyed about the top 10 changes they observed among young people today. Their most common responses (followed by the number of individuals who gave this response) are these:

1. The number of dysfunctional families has grown. (35)
2. High technology has influenced school, work, and home life. (21)
3. Children are threatened by crime, violence, ignorance, and poverty. (19)
4. Communities are changing, becoming more diverse. (19)
5. Mass media grips our children (17), giving them more knowledge (14) at an earlier age. (11)
6. Students question authority and shun traditional values, responsibilities. (16)
7. A hurry-up society often lacks a sense of community. (12)
8. Changing workplaces create demands for higher levels of literacy. (12)
9. Knowledge about learning styles demands new kinds of education. (10)
10. Peers exert a powerful influence on values. (10)

In addition to the major (and interrelated) changes listed above, 10 or more finalists identified these factors as having changed greatly for students over the last 40 years: activities, mobility, poverty, language, readiness, sports, and tolerance. Some of these will be touched on briefly throughout the text of this book.

The Good, the Bad, and the Unbearable

Here's the good news. Statistics confirm that not all of what's happening to students is bad, and the bad things are not happening to all students:

- In 1992, 87 percent of 19- and 20-year-olds had earned a high school credential.
- The dropout rate has declined steadily during the past 20 years.
- College attendance has increased from 4 million to 15 million since 1977.
- Average math and science achievement for 9-, 13-, and 17-year-olds has increased since 1982, according to the National Assessment of Educational Progress.
- U.S. students rank favorably in reading achievement, compared with international competitors, according to 1995 education indicators from the Organization for Economic Cooperation and Development.
- SAT scores for all ethnic groups except whites, have risen since 1975.[1]

> *"Schools have become mom, dad, church, and community. It's a Catch 22. We're at the point where before we can educate kids, we have to peel off the problems from the night before."*
>
> *—Kenneth Burnley, superintendent, Colorado Springs, Colorado*

However,

- In 1993, we had more than 14.6 million children living in poverty, including 22.7 percent of children under 18, and nearly three times that of our international competitors, according to the Economic Policy Institute.
- High school completion rates were substantially lower for Hispanics (65 percent) and blacks (81 percent) than for whites (90 percent) in 1992.
- In 1991, American students scored lower than students in Korea, Switzerland, and Taiwan in a mathematics assessment and lower than students in Hungary, Korea, and Taiwan in three out of four areas tested in science, according to the International Assessment of Educational Progress.
- 78 percent of students have cheated.[2]
- 29 percent have considered suicide.[3]
- One in four schools is vandalized each month.
- An estimated 270,000 guns are carried to school each day, according to the U.S. Justice Department.

1 Gerald W. Bracey, *Transforming America's Schools: An Rx For Getting Past Blame*, 1994, pps. 9-10, American Association of School Administrators.
2 Education Life, p. 12, The New York Times, January 8, 1995.
3 Ibid., p. 12.

- 35 percent of students surveyed said they would engage in sex without a condom.[4]
- The number of births to unmarried teens increased 32.7 percent between 1980 and 1990. (*Shattering Stereotypes: A Demographic Look at Children in the United States*, Institute for Educational Leadership, Inc., 1001 Connecticut Ave., NW, Suite 310, Washington, DC 20036.)
- The number of teenagers and young adults with AIDS increased by more than 75 percent between 1990-92, and AIDS is now the sixth-leading cause of death among youth ages 13-24.[5]
- Student drug use increased significantly during the 1990s, with 27 percent of 10th-graders reporting illicit drug use in 1993.
- Children watch 5,000 hours of television by the first grade and 19,000 hours by the end of high school — more time than they spend in class.[6]
- Gangs, once a phenomenon in only urban areas, were a factor in incidents of school violence in 27 percent of cities with populations under 50,000, according to a 1994 survey by the National League of Cities.
- From 1986 to 1991, the number of youths and teenagers killed by firearms rose 59 percent, from 3,373 to 5,356 annually, according to the FBI.[7]
- Homicide is the most common cause of death for young African American males.

Donning Doc Martens, engineer motorcycle boots, baggy jeans and baby doll dresses, Sony Walkmans, and paging devices, today's students may be every marketer's dream. They will eclipse the baby boomers' numbers by the year 2010, both in population size and longevity. But, the oft-maligned latchkey, video- and techno-literate younger generation are—for many of us—angst, anger, and attitude rolled into one. (See Figure 1.)

The following chapter will explore each of five groups of changes derived from the superintendent's top 10 list.

What's On Teens' Minds?

A 1994 study by Teenage Research Unlimited found young people grappling with these issues:

1. AIDS
2. Education
3. Race relations
4. Violence
5. Abortion
6. Child abuse
7. The environment
8. Drinking and driving
9. Drug abuse
10. The economy

---

4 Ibid., p. 12.
5 The House Select Committee on Children, Youth and Families, April, 1992.
6 Mortimer B. Zuckerman, "The Victims of TV Violence," p. 64, *U.S. News & World Report*, August 2, 1993.
7 Bill Moyers, "There's So Much We Can Do," p. 5, January 8, 1995, *Parade Magazine*, Parade Publications, New York, New York.

Figure 1: Select Generational Characteristics

Dependables (Pre-1940s - '40s)	Pushies (Baby boomers) ('50s and '60s)	Standbys ('70s - present)
Old-time religion	Spiritualism Consciousness revolution	Pragmatic
Shalls/shall nots	"Do your own thing"	"What is my thing?"
Science	Questioning	Ecology/pollution
Patience	Impatience Instant gratification	Overload frustration
Puritan, uptight	Free love, experimental	Cybersex, casual
Optimistic	Pessimistic	Resigned, cynical
Formal dress code	Informal dress code	Non-descript, blah
Conformity: "Yes, sir!"	Nonconformity: "Why?"	Diversity: "Why not?"
Rules, roles, regulations	Questioning	Confrontative
Prescribed	Personal experiences	Media-savvy, street-smart
Family, community	Self-centered, materialistic	Think globally, act locally
Responsible, stable	Non-responsible, searching	Selectively responsible
Class conscious	Self-conscious	Democratic
Builders, doers	Critics	Repair crew
Spare rod, spoil child	Dr. Spock	Latchkey
Values specific	Values flux/breakdown	Values vacuum
Seriously serious	Unseriously serious	Seriously unserious
"Pro"	"Anti-"	Variable
Avoid unpleasants	Confront issues	Open, realistic

Source: Morris Massey Associates, Boulder, Colorado.

Part Two:

The Five Groups Of Changes

1. Clan Connections

A child's values are imprinted before the age of 7, through family, the media, religion, income, and geographical location. During this time, children learn the difference between right and wrong, good and bad, normal and abnormal.

—Morris Massey, Morris Massey Associates, Boulder, Colorado, Just Get It, *1995 (videotape)*

The Family: From "Nuclear" to "Unclear"

Like the superintendents surveyed for this book, students believe the "decline of the family" to be the most significant phenomena occurring today. Moreover, they believe the "family crisis" is more important than crime and environmental pollution.[8] The recession, coupled with the social upheaval in the family and other institutions in the 1980s, took

8 *Who's Who Among American High School Students,*" November 16, 1994, Educational Communications, Inc., Lake Forest, Illinois.

its toll on many Americans. To make ends meet, single parents often work two jobs, and often, where there are two parents, both work. Though some parents turn to home-based businesses to be close to their children, the majority still spend a large part of their lives at work and away from their children, often adding long commutes on top of long days. According to the Family Research Council, parents spend just 17 waking hours a week with their children, in contrast to 30 hours in 1965.

A growing number, but still comparatively few employers have such family-friendly policies as on-site day care, family leave, job-sharing, flex-time, telecommuting, and time off for community service. Families are under pressure and children are paying the price.

These statistics show that all too many children grow up without the support, guidance, and discipline they need to make responsible choices.

Human interaction — family, church, and community — is the basis for learning what it takes to become a decent person. Until recently, children contributed to the "survival, protection, and well-being of the clan," says Dr. Bernard Z. Friedlander of the University of Hartford's Department of Psychology. Their sense of self and place in the family and in the community was secure, clear, understandable, and valued.

"If we pass the job of minding the kids on to the TV set, if we fail to listen actively to what they have to say or to hold them accountable for their actions, we deprive them of what they need to know to build decent futures — for themselves and for everybody else," adds Friedlander.

Dysfunctional families

"The term `dysfunction' has lost much of its meaning because of its overuse," says Katherine Smith, a clinical psychologist with the Family Therapy Institute in Alexandria, Virginia. "But basically, in a dysfunctional family, there is a recurring pattern of a member (or members) of the family who does not support (or even impedes) the emotional, psychological, spiritual, or physical growth of its members, including themselves."

Kids from dysfunctional families may suffer not only physical abuse but also emotional neglect. "The dysfunctional family has given many youngsters fewer roots upon which to grow," says Albert Eads Jr., superintendent, Estill, South Carolina. Children growing up in these families often exhibit symptoms ranging from withdrawal and depression to indifference, resignation, cynicism, aggression, truancy, poor grades, drug and alcohol abuse, and other negative behaviors.

Dysfunctional families, coupled with the poverty so often associated with them, often spawn children who are physically and emotionally unhealthy and not ready for the challenges of formal schooling.

Unfortunately, too, the poor do not always seek help available to them to give students a boost. According to the U.S. General Accounting Office, 11 percent of the 4.6 million parents on Aid to Families with Dependent Children (AFDC) do not participate in any of the education, training, or job search programs set up by the 1988 Family Support Act.

The effect on children

The National Association of School Nurses reports that incidents of clinical depression appear to be growing among young children.[9] One Maryland high school even devoted a day to talking to students about depression, complete with a visit from representatives of the manufacturer of Prozac, the hot-selling drug of the '90s.

Even among junior- and senior-year high school students who are earning A's or B's,

---

9 The Basic School by Ernest Boyer, 1995, Carnegie Foundation for the Advancement of Teaching.

No Safety At the Top

A 1995 study published by "Who's Who Among American High School Students" found evidence that even top students are prone to disturbing behavior:

- Almost one-third (29 percent) of the 3,100 high-achieving students surveyed said they had considered suicide—up from 17 percent in 1971.
- 78 percent admitted to cheating—up from 70 percent in 1983.
- More high-achieving students are admitting to driving after drinking alcohol—21 percent, up from only 7 percent surveyed in 1983.

However:

- Only 10 percent said they had tried marijuana, down from 27 percent in 1972.
- Almost all (91 percent) top achievers said they used contraceptives when sexually active, up from 52 percent in 1972.

Interestingly, confidence in government and the media is on the wane among high achievers: In 1971, 31 percent of those taking part in the Who's Who survey had a "great deal" of confidence in the president—today only 11 percent said they do. Similarly, only 5 percent said they had confidence in the media as opposed to 20 percent in 1971.

"The nation's top high school students are in many ways quite different from their predecessors 25 years ago—they seem more cynical, more mature, and for better and worse, more adult."

—*Renee Sanchez, "Survey Finds Maturity, Cynicism Among High-Achieving Teens,"* The Washington Post, *June 15, 1995.*

who plan to attend college, and who believe their family life to be happy and close, there is cause for concern. Paul Krouse, publisher of "Who's Who Among American High School Students" and "The National Dean's List" (ECI) cautions, "Parents need to know that the moment their off-spring reach the top of the heap is still no time to relax. The strongest guarantee that these kids will live up to their potential is to have parents they can turn to."[10]

The Dynamics of a Changing Demographic Mix

Of the total of 258 million Americans, 20 million were born in another country. However, one in three teenagers belongs to a minority group ("Teens — Here Comes the Biggest Wave Yet," *Business Week*, April 11, 1994). In some communities, the language barrier is great. Barbara Devlin, superintendent in Villa Park, Illinois, reports students in her schools speak more than 38 languages at home. And, Kenneth Moffett, 1994 National Superintendent of the Year, reports that 90 percent of his kindergarten pupils in Lennox, California, speak no English at all.

Figure 2 below illustrates our changing demographic composition:

Figure 2:
Estimated and Projected School-Age Population
By Race and Ethnicity

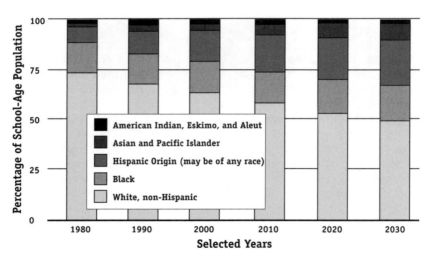

Source: U.S. Bureau of the Census (1993), Population Projections of the United States, by Age, Sex, Race, and Hispanic Origin, 1993 to 2030, Series P25-1104, pp. xxv-xxxvi; U.S. Bureau of the Census (1993) Statistical Abstract of the United States, 1993, p. 22.

---

10 Ibid., p. 4.

Greater tolerance

In Essex Junction, Vermont, superintendent Raymond Proulx notes that today's students encourage one another to express cultural pride through music, language, art, and dress.

In the Palominas School District of rural southeastern Arizona, students participate in Hands Across the Border, a cross-cultural exchange between Mexico and the United States. Superintendent Gene Brust says kids learn quickly that "national boundaries, cultural differences, economic and ethnic diversities, and unfamiliar family structures are unimportant compared to bonds of friendship, respect, and understanding."

But one doesn't have to cross international boundaries to build cross-cultural understanding. New York City's Educators for Social Responsibility's Resolving Conflicts Creatively Program (RCCP), Project STOP, and Multicultural Education Project (MEP) teach students that words and understanding are more effective than violence in resolving conflicts and that "difference" and "diversity" can be sources of commonality and strength.

"Schools with healthy relations among diverse students don't shy away from the issue of diversity and differences," according to John O'Neil of the Association for Supervision and Curriculum Development. Indeed, most of the superintendents agreed today's students are more tolerant of people of different racial, ethnic, and cultural groups than students were in the 1960s. Both boys and girls appear to embrace gender equality as well. Schools deserve much of the credit — multicultural curricula, conflict resolution or mediation skill-building, and cooperative learning have contributed to the growing tolerance among today's students.

Racial strife continues. Still, there is racial strife in schools, and more than anyone cares to admit, says Ronald Stephens, executive director of the National School Safety Center. There were 120 reported racial incidents in schools between December, 1991; and February 15, 1992, accross 25 states.[11]

"It's now the school's task to overcome communication barriers and cultural biases. Pride in one's self and in one's culture and self-esteem are issues that need to be addressed," says Stan Paz, superintendent, El Paso, Texas.

"The challenge to public educators," says Ernest Husark, superintendent in Westerville, Ohio, "is to help acquaint the student with his community without sacrificing the student's identity — to consider diversity a strength, not a threat."

Loss of Community

The cocoon of family and community is now more fragile than ever. What of the butterfly? Superintendent Theresa Kisor in Piedmont, Alaska,

---

11 John O'Neil, "A New Generation Confronts Racism," *Educational Leadership*, May, 1993, p. 61.

says, "Our social institutions have left our children without the necessary support to grow and develop within a framework of love and caring."

Today's students, says Tom Maes, superintendent in Adams County, Colorado, no longer live in a single locality but, instead, "in the entire world." From "The Simpsons" and "Beavis and Butt-Head," to Bosnia, the Los Angeles riots, and crime on the nightly news, the mass media sell violence as a means of resolving conflict, sexuality as power, negative stereotypes, self-absorption, and vulgar language to our children. Absent greater family and community involvement and guidance, these are the "norms" our students come to accept, value, and embody.

2. Disconnect!

Endangered: Respect, Accountability, Responsibility

Many argue that today's students are growing more disconnected from their families, their communities, and even from themselves. They seem to feel they are entitled to success, rather than having to earn it. And when they don't become successful, they claim they are victims of a society that has turned its back on them. This attitude transcends racial, ethnic and gender lines, and is further evidence of our cultural crisis, our moral laxity, some believe.

"To create a fulfilling emotional life...we must recognize three basic requirements of any individual: the needs for community, structure, and meaning. ...Community offsets loneliness. It gives a vitally necessary sense of belonging. Yet, today, the institutions on which community depends are crumbling in all the techno-societies. The result is a spreading plague of loneliness."

—Alvin Toffler,
Coda: The Great Influence:
"The Attack on Loneliness,"
The Third Wave, 1990, p. 367

Shared blame. Adults bear some of the responsibility for this perspective. We value materialism, money, and fame over public service and provide few positive role models for our children. Even in the courtroom we devalue personal responsibility. Witness the widespread use of pleas of temporary insanity; or blaming junk food, television, or urban stress syndrome for mayhem and murder.

Many of today's students enter the job market lacking the work ethic that characterized young people in years past. As one businessman in Bethesda, Maryland, put it:

Our interns are self-absorbed and disrespectful of others. It's apparent in their language, in their dress, in their behavior, and in the quality of their work. We're a team here. We do what we have to do, even if it means xeroxing a four-hundred page proposal on a

Friday evening. Their (students') only concern seems to be 'what's in it for me.' I don't know, maybe I just don't get it . . .

Superintendent Richard Kendell, of Farmington, Utah, adds that this "flight from personal responsibility" is a serious problem for our country. "It seems to me today's students feel others are the cause of their lack of success," echoes Carolyn Dumaresq, superintendent, Harrisburg, Pennsylvania.

Superintendent Kenneth Burnley of Colorado Springs, Colorado, says, "In a society where the individual is emphasized over the group, where sports stars are paid exorbitant salaries, where lawsuits erupt over the flimsiest of reasons, it's hardly surprising our kids mirror society."

Peer Group Influence

A child's peer group exerts increasing influence in the later years of elementary school and beyond. At this stage, children have a need to find out where they belong or fit outside of the context of the family. Parents must learn to tolerate peer group involvement so their children can expand their horizons. But, when a child is unduly influenced by her peer group, it likely means she is "spiraling out of the family because she is not getting what she needs at home — support, understanding, and a sense of belonging," says Katherine Smith, clinical psychologist in Virginia.

Group dating. Dating has changed quite a bit since the '50s and '60s. Teens tend to meet in groups and conduct their dating life within a circle of friends until a relationship becomes serious.

The lure of gangs. Children join gangs to satisfy their "need to belong," adds Capt. Vince McInerney, a police officer in Kansas City, Missouri. But seeking out such a substitute for family can prove to be a lethal choice. What sets today's gangs apart from those of yesterday is the availability of weapons, the propensity to use them indiscriminately, and the proliferation of drugs (both for use and sale), McInerney says.

"In my 20 years as a teacher and 10 as a counselor, I see greater anger, depression, fear, and rage. Because of the pressure on parents ...they don't spend enough time with their kids. Kids learn a range of inappropriate emotional vocabulary from the television. What's sad is the loss of human interaction, loss of touch with nature, and the loss of community. Their emotional skills are just not there!"

—Barbara Johnson, counselor, Bertha Reid Elementary School, Thornton, Colorado

"One of the things that really concerns me about the divorce rate in a community like mine is not the husbands and wives. They'll hurt, but they'll survive.... I'm really afraid we are raising a generation of children who will be afraid to love."

—Rabbi Harold S. Kushner, senior rabbi, Temple Israel, Natick, Massachusetts Dennis Wholey, Are You Happy?, Houghton-Mifflin Company, Boston, Massachusetts , 1986, p. 14

According to Kenneth Moffett, 1994 National Superintendent of the Year from Lennox, California, "Their loyalty, their bottom line, is to that gang. Once they're there, they'll do anything they can to stay there. Along about age 9 or 10, they start shooting to prove they belong." From his own experience he knows schools can have safe campuses even in the presence of gangs: "Our campus is safe — even with nine gangs — because the gangs know their younger brothers and sisters are there. No gang labels, no gang signs."

The real thing. In short, children recognize and feel the distinction between sandwiched-in "quality time" and genuine concern, guidance, and nurturing. If the child hasn't learned self-coping and conflict resolution skills, then he is susceptible to acting out, through rage, violence, vandalism, drugs, alcohol, eating disorders, or other forms of self-abuse.

A more optimistic view is espoused by T. Berry Brazelton, professor emeritus of pediatrics at Harvard Medical School and founder and chief of the Child Development University at Boston's Children's Hospital. "Despite the very real power of peers in the elementary grades, the family is still the primary influence in a child's life. Peer pressure grows more powerful, but a strong foundation—and the support of parents who are willing to be a little flexible and who know where to draw the line—can counter even negative influences," he says.

The Pressure Cooker: Student Activities and Performance

Parents tend to schedule activity after activity for their children, rather than leaving them unsupervised after school. Organized play has turned a leisurely game of softball into a win-at-all-costs activity.

"Every afternoon, scores of children rush from school to ballet, soccer practice, math enrichment centers, music, gymnastics, swim, football, modeling, hockey, chorus, and karate classes. A lot of these kids have schedules you or I would struggle with," says Hans Steiner, director of the division of Psychiatry at Lucille Packard Children's Hospital at Stanford. "Some kids love competition and the challenges of these activities, but, sometimes the greater need being served by this focused activity is not the child's, but the parent's.

"We've coached kids to death, with summer camps, weight training, viewing videos. It's very rare you see a group of young people playing softball with no supervision," says Dennis Kimzey, superintendent, Dillon, Montana.

"We asked these kids to describe the worst thing that had happened to them in the last year," explains Steiner in an article in *Children's Ink* titled "Kids and Stress: How Parents Can Help."

"The majority of the complaints involved increasing performance anxiety....One boy described the reaction of his father when the boy scored in the 99th percentile for reading ability on a standardized test. The father wanted to know why not 100," recalls Steiner.

> *This search for meaning and for belonging "ends in the total subjugation of self" — in, for example, racial/ethnic factionalism, reactionaryism, nationalism and religious fundamentalism, suicide, drug and alcohol abuse, violence, and membership in ersatz families such as cults and gangs.'"*
>
> —Richard Eckersley, "The West's Deepening Cultural Crisis," The Futurist, December, 1993, p. 12

3. Plugged In

The Influence of the Media

Though some accuse parents of scheduling their children out of time to relax; more prevalent, perhaps, are hours children spend watching uninterrupted television. It has become the electronic baby-sitter in some families, even with the violence and sex that now permeate the tube. After 35 years of research on the effect of television on children, Leonard Eron, research professor emeritus, University of Illinois at Chicago and former chair of the American Psychological Association's Commission on Violence and Youth, says there "can no longer be any doubt that heavy exposure to televised violence is one of the causes of aggressive behavior, crime, and violence in society."[12] Moreover, those watching the least television tended to perform better on standardized tests. (See Figure 3.)

Although a negative correlation appears to exist between television watching and performance on achievement tests, other variables such as socioeconomic characteristics also are related to television viewing and achievement. Higher socioeconomic students were less likely to watch five or more hours of TV on school nights and more likely to have high test scores than low socioeconomic students.

---

12 Louise Sweeney, "Research Links Violence on TV with Aggression," *Christian Science Monitor*, April 7, 1992.

Figure 3: T.V. and Test Performance

Percentage of high school sophomores who watch more than five hours of television on school nights, by test performance and socioeconomic status: 1990

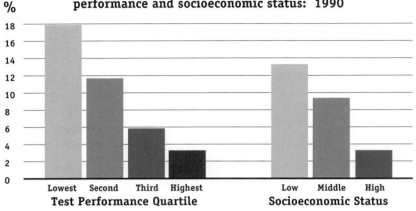

Source: U.S. Department of Education. National Center for Education Statistics. National Education Longitudinal Study of 1988. "First Followup" survey.

M(ind-numbing) TV. Most at risk are pre-adolescents who may not distinguish between fantasy and reality. By elementary school age, kids have watched 8,000 murders on television! Hardly the stuff of childhood. According to George Gerbner, a researcher at the University of Pennsylvania, there are now 26.4 violent acts per hour on children's programs.[13] MTV's mid-1990s "Beavis and Butt-Head" and other animated shows depict characters whose main pleasure in life is watching television.

Educators believe the knowledge explosion, lack of respect, materialism, and violence characteristic of some young people have their roots in television.

To be fair... Not all television is bad, of course. Nor can we attribute antisocial behavior solely to television. "Sesame Street," "Bill Nye the Science Guy," "Lamb Chop's Play-Along," "Where in the World is Carmen San Diego," and "Mister Rogers" were but a few of the responsible programs on TV when this book was published. Notably, all are products of public broadcasting. But there are afternoon teen specials on the networks that alert

> *"I played football, basketball, and base-ball freshman year... I just couldn't deal with their attitude and it was always Win, Win, Win... I basically quit sports because of that attitude."*
>
> —*Male, Darien High School, Connecticut, Border Crossing, 1994, created by the students of Norwalk, New Canaan, and Darien school districts and funded by the state of Connecticut*

---

13 Karen L. Bauer, "TV murder and mayhem: How do they affect our kids?" *PTA Today*, May/June, 1994.

students to the dangers of HIV-AIDS and drug and alcohol abuse, as well as educational programs on The Discovery and Learning Channels.

Meanwhile, TV executives have long argued television is a harmless escape. People with guns cause violence, not television, they argue. TV merely reflects society, they add.

Fighting back. However, under the Television Violence Act, the networks have initiated a parental advisory rating system and joint standards.

Spearheading the anti-violence movement is the Center for Media Literacy (CML) based in Los Angeles, California, with its "Beyond Blame: Challenging Violence in the Media" multimedia program. Through CML, schools, churches, and community groups have marshaled their efforts to promote media literacy.

Parents for Peace in Compton, California, for example, designed workshops in violence in the media, conflict resolution, and communication skills. The National Alliance for Non-Violent Programming, Minneapolis-based Turn Off the Violence, and the Anti-Violence Task Force of the North Shore Congregation Israel in Glencoe, Illinois, are working to educate parents, teachers, and students about bias and violence in the media. Still, it's up to parents to limit and monitor their children's TV diet if we are to make any headway in educating our children. (See "Helping Students Become Media Literate," p. 36.)

Violence in music and video games
Romanticizing death is back in music and other venues, as well. In the 1990s, bands such as Megadeath, Nine Inch Nails, and Nirvana (Kurt Cobain, the lead singer, committed suicide) pushed anomie, ennui, desperation, defiance, and hopelessness to the edge. Defiance, crassness, sex, aggression, and violence are not limited, however, to television, alternative rock, and "Gangsta Rap" music; they permeate the video and computer gaming industry as well.

Remote control
Mass media affect behavior by influencing the development of an individual's cognitive scripts. Susceptibility to a given message, however, depends on the individual's home environment, interests, needs, and concerns. Admonishes Barry Sanders, a teacher at the Claremont College in Pasadena, California, "We may be creating a new kind of human being...Television creates the remotest kind of behavior."[14]

The Knowledge Explosion and Earlier Adulthood

Some believe that fractured families and daily exposure to stressors such as environmental disasters, war, starvation, AIDS, poverty, abuse of power, and drug and crime stories on the nightly news have fostered adolescents who are old before their time.

---

14 "Does TV Kill?" *Frontline*, Public Broadcasting Service, January 9-11, 1995.

What is the danger of hurrying children to become adults before they are emotionally ready? Most adolescent behavior researchers believe children become more susceptible to premature sexual relations, drugs, alcohol, and negative peer group influence. Says Dale Mabe, superintendent, Meridian, Idaho, kids are "information rich but experience poor," demanding relevancy in their studies. In other words, they've seen it all, they may think they "know it all," but they don't necessarily know what to do with the information they have. Educators need to both make schooling relevant to their lives and give young people guidance as to how to use the learning they receive to live most productively and positively.

The Influence of Technology

Students today have taken to technology with amazing ease, leaving many of their elders in the dust.

In a keystroke, we can access information and participate in discussion groups across time and space borders. Cyberdemocracy and cyberspace grip the American public's imagination, and computers can indeed be powerful learning tools. However, the "gods" of numbers, efficiency, and speed threaten to devalue and atomize meaningful forms of human connection, writes Neil Postman, in *Technopoly*.[15] He warns, we must take great care not to diminish the value of our essential "human" and "spiritual" nature and needs.

Mindful of these perils, most educators agree that computers in the classroom hold great promise when used properly. Sophisticated computers — with databases, spreadsheets, word processing, internet, and multimedia capability — free students from laborious tasks, enhance their creativity, boost their interest and attention levels, and even promote teamwork.

Authentic, cooperative, and distance learning; cross-age mentoring (i.e., "generation to generation"); greater interactivity through CD-ROM and videodisc multimedia; and direct access to the latest research are revolutionizing how students learn. Learning via computer is more fluid and personalized than the traditional predigested textbook-driven curricula. Students experience the joy of discovery — of owning their ideas. The emphasis shifts from knowledge-as-product to knowledge-as-process.

According to a report by the National Association of Secondary School Principals,

> The ability of technology to allow new methods of learning and instruction will greatly alter many of our current concepts of what a school should be and how it should operate....Teachers who can inspire, motivate, guide, create, and manage the educational progress of their students will be in demand...Communication will be the most important skill: communication with other people,

---

15 Neil Postman, *Technopoly*, Vintage Books, New York, 1993.

with computers and technology, with other ideas and cultures, with related process and techniques. ("Technology in the Classroom: Planning for Educational Change," *Curriculum Report*, March 1993)

Learning Styles:
Customer-Focused, Flexible, and Fun

Superintendent Josephine Kelleher, Woonsocket, Rhode Island, reports students' ability to concentrate on one task for long periods has been replaced by an aptitude for processing several messages simultaneously. And, reports Iowa's Gary Wegenke, in addition to the preference for non-linear thinking, students seem to like to "discuss the information with classmates and collaboratively address problems."

"Today's students want more flexibility," says William Adams, superintendent, Woodstown, New Jersey, "but, they also want structure. They want to know `why.'"

Teachers are, by and large, excited about the more interactive formats that address different learning styles and make them the "guide on the side" rather than the "sage on the stage." It's imperative to provide teachers with the training they need to become motivators and mentors, however. This "coaching" type of teaching is not easy for all staff and should be taught like any other skill.

> *"We can no longer operate under the illusion that we can provide all the needs and skills students will need for the 21st Century. Schools must devote greater effort to help students use their minds and become literate users of developing technologies."*
>
> —Herbert Torres, superintendent, Silver City, New Mexico

4. Unplugged!

From the Hood to the 'Burbs and the Hills

"Fasten your seat belts," says James Fox, a professor of criminology at Northeastern University. "The country is in for a violent crime wave as the number of teenagers increases by 23 percent over the next decade."[16] Even once halcyon rural areas have not been spared. Eighty-two percent of the 720 school districts surveyed in 1994 by the National School Boards Association reported an increase in violence; 78 percent were student-on-student assaults and 28 percent, student-on-teacher attacks.[17]

---

16 "Young, Angry, and Lethal," *Newsweek*, January 2, 1995, p. 122.
17 Jessica Portner, "School Violence Up Over Past 5 Years, 82% in Survey Say," *Education Week*, January 12, 1994, p. 9.

According to the American Psychological Association, teenagers are two and one-half times as likely to be victims of violent crimes as people over 20."[18] Figures 4 and 5 below illustrate the impact of youth violent crime and its causes.

Figure 4
Percent Increases By Crime
(1988-92)

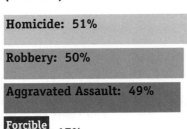

Figure 5
Family Breakdown Blamed

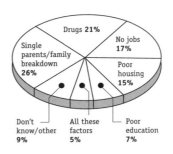

Source: FBI Uniform Crime reports; Poll from The National Journal, *Aug. 8, 1994, by J.L. Albert,* USA Today, *September 28, 1994.*

One problem is that students arm themselves for protection against gangs and other violent students, says Omaha's assistant police chief Larry Rogers, on the force for 20 years. Now teenagers throughout the area try to match the firepower of the gang members. "If one kid brings a .22 caliber pistol and the other has a 357 Magnum, then guess who has the status?" Rogers says.

Solitary Confinement

While our perception of crime and violence has most certainly been fueled by the media, violence is part of life for many young people. Fearing for their children's safety, parents have gone beyond arming their kids with beepers; they've confined them to their homes and proscribed their social activities. But, in social confinement, or "lockdown," as the teenagers call it, parents run the risk of creating "strangers in their own world," says Dalton Miller Jones, a professor of developmental psychology at Portland State University, in Oregon.

"In many communities, the school is the only safe spot students have to get away from violence," says Carol Grosse-Peck, superintendent of Alhambra School District in Phoenix, Arizona, and former National Superintendent of the Year. Many schools have made safety a priority.

---

18 DeNeen L. Brown, "Afraid to Die, Afraid to Live," *The Washington Post*, January 16, 1995, A1, A8.

They have:

- Developed strict discipline and enforcement procedures.
- Banned gang clothing and insignias.
- Restricted the use of school facilities after hours.
- Issued ID cards to students.
- Armed teachers with beepers and set up emergency response teams.
- Banned race/ethnic insignias.
- Instituted mandatory multicultural education courses.
- Established conflict resolution programs for students.
- Held neighborhood peace conferences with local government officials, members of the community, and police department.
- Installed metal detectors and surveillance cameras.
- Required students to wear school uniforms.
- Increased the visibility of security guards.
- Removed lockers to prevent weapon and drug concealment.

For example, the Prince George's County, Maryland, school district began a Shock Mentor Program, where students visit the trauma and emergency rooms in hospitals to watch doctors patch up victims and perpetrators of violence. Many schools have found peer mentoring programs successful as well. But, there are other problems too. . .

"I feel society has begun to accept violence as the norm. This acceptance of violence as commonplace, coupled with the availability of guns on the street, places our youth in a perilous position, both as perpetrators of crime and as victims.... The prevalent attitude today seems to be, 'what can life do for me,' and, if there is a problem, 'who can I find to be responsible for this and who is going to take care of me?,...I saw this at a scene of a recent homicide in Kansas City (Missouri) which involved a teenage victim who was involved with drugs. As friends gathered around the scene, one of the young men said, 'this is going to keep happening as long as we're out on the street. Someone better find some place for us to go and give us something to do....They have no conception of personal responsibility nor do they have the willingness to do anything to help themselves."

—Captain Vince McInerney,
Commander,
Media Relations Office
Kansas City, Missouri,
Police Department

Between 1983 and 1993, the murder rate among boys ages 14 to 17 more than doubled. Beginning in 1985, boys in this age group began to be recruited into the lucrative crack cocaine trade where violent turf wars are common.

—"Gun Ownership Rises Steadily,
and Murder Rate for
Young Men Doubles,"
Health, The Washington Post,
January 3, 1995, p. 12

The Other War Zone: Drugs and Alcohol

According to the U.S. Department of Health and Human Services "Monitoring the Future" report and the University of Michigan at Ann Arbor's 1993 survey of 50,000 8th-, 10th-, and 12th-grade students across the country, drug use is on the rise. Between 1993 and 1994, the number of young people reporting they use marijuana rose to 13 percent of 8th-graders (+50 percent), 25 percent of 10th-graders (+33 percent), and 31 percent of 12th-graders (+40 percent). Heroin, LSD, and powder and crack cocaine also are on the rise, but not as sharply as marijuana. Inhalants (the latest rage), alcohol, and cigarettes also are popular among teenagers.

Why the rise in drug use? Here are a few reasons:

- Dysfunctional families
- Negative influence of peer groups and gangs
- Self-expression
- Defiance
- Feelings of hopelessness, frustration, and depression
- Sense of invulnerability
- Lack of sense of responsibility — sense of victimization
- Ease of access
- The lure of money from drug dealing.

Lloyd Johnston, survey leader at the University of Michigan, believes glamorization of violence and drugs in the music industry also is partly to blame. "Various rap and grunge groups talk about drugs and are open about their own use." [19]

Red Ribbons/Red Flags: The Battleground of the Human Body

While early sexuality has always held potentially serious consequences for teenagers, only since the early '80s have sex and death been equated so closely.

A 1993 Center for Disease Control survey reported 68,000 people aged 20-29 had been diagnosed with AIDS, which means they likely contracted the virus in their teens. Indeed, the AIDS virus can take as long as 10 years

---

19 Tom Friend, "Pot use in high school up sharply," *USA Today*, December 13, 1994.

to be diagnosed. What's worse, nearly a fifth of all high school students said they had four or more sex partners.[20]

Starting early

The average age for a girl in the U.S. to engage in sexual intercourse for the first time is 16; for a boy, 15.5.[21] Moreover, only 46 percent of high school students reported using a condom during their last sexual intercourse. Unfortunately, there are now 3 million reported cases of American teenagers with a sexually transmitted disease (STD). And, because nearly 60 percent of all high school students have used illegal drugs, those sharing needles and syringes are especially at risk of contracting AIDS.[22]

The U.S. Department of Health and Human Services, "HIV/AIDS Surveillance Report, of June, 1994, found HIV infectious cases (not AIDS) highest among the males. However, the tide has changed over the last decade: Girls are at greater risk for contracting HIV/AIDS than boys.

Children having babies. One-third of all babies born in the United States are born to unwed mothers. One in seven babies is born to a teenager. — John Hockenberry, *Day One*, February 16, 1995, (ABC).

"I used to stomp girls, push girls in the face. If they looked at me hard, I used to beat them up....[our conflict-resolution teacher] changed me. Telling me about listening, about respect. Here, everybody takes classes in conflict resolution. And you gotta sign a contract that you won't fight."

—Janet Gonzales, 19, New York City, mediator, Resolving Conflict Creatively Program, the Bronx, New York, Bill Moyers, "There Is So Much We Can Do," Parade Magazine, January 8, 1995, p. 6

Young girls are becoming pregnant at earlier ages. More disturbing, many of these pregnancies are by choice. And, just like crime, the phenomenon of teen pregnancy is not limited to urban neighborhoods.

Though schools and community agencies offer sex education courses and counseling for teen mothers, and in some cases, day care on school grounds, more and more teens are becoming parents despite the personal and financial hardships they face, and many are forced to go on welfare to support their children.

Sadly, studies show that teens who are on welfare at an early age are more likely to be on welfare longer. What is the cost to us? In 1992, teen pregnancies cost the U.S. taxpayer $32 billion including health care costs associated with low-birthweight and premature babies, welfare and other social services. In sum, the choices our teens make affect us all.

---

20 World AIDS Day, 1994 — AIDS and Families, "AIDS in the United States," American Association for World Health, 1994, p. 19, provided by the Whitman Walker Clinic, Washington, D.C.
21 "What is HIV Infection? And What is AIDS?" *AIDS PREVENTION GUIDE*, Center for Disease Control, U.S. Department of Health & Human Services.
22 "What is HIV Infection? And What is AIDS?" *AIDS PREVENTION GUIDE*, Center for Disease Control, U.S. Department of Health & Human Services.

The other great depression

Depression also seems to characterize today's students. One in five adolescents was diagnosed with a mental disorder in 1993. The percentage of teens who have attempted suicide at least once rose from 6 percent in 1988 to 13 percent in 1993. In fact, suicide ranked as the third leading cause of death among children and adolescents in 1993.

Acceptance, belonging, and self-esteem

Literally dying for acceptance, self-worth, and belonging, many teens turn to or away from food to solve their problems. Bombarded by advertisements and pressured by their peers, teens suffer from anorexia nervosa and bulimia, two eating disorders (sometimes fatal) that play havoc with the body's chemistry and brain function.

Trying to emulate fashion models like Kate Moss, the model who refashioned the Twiggy look of the '60s to the waif look of the '90s, many young girls starve themselves for attention and approval (anorexia nervosa). Others resort to binging and purging, known as bulimia. With more than 30 years of research on eating disorders, experts now know that they often are the result of family dysfunction. Eating disorders, like so many other negative behaviors, are a clarion call for "I want to be loved. I want you to think I'm okay."

5. High Hopes or Future Shock?

The Myth?

The following statistics from two surveys of high school seniors conducted by the National Center for Education Statistics: the National Longitud-

---

23 "The Agony of Adolescents," *Psychology Today*, May-June, 1993, p. 18.

inal Survey of 1972 (NLS) and the National Education Longitudinal Study of 1988 (NELS:88), 1992 Second Followup, indicate high school seniors are relatively positive in their outlook and expectations for the future.

For example, both male and female high school seniors expect to enter managerial and professional fields. Moreover, female high school seniors expecting to enter clerical positions declined dramatically, from 25.5 percent in 1972 to 5.7 percent in 1992. Clearly, communities and schools have made great strides in leveling the playing field for young women. In addition, the data show a decline in expectation for entering the service field among both male and female high school seniors, though low-pay service sector jobs are holding steady.

The Reality...

Expecting to get a job is one thing, but getting a traditional full-time, on-site job with a regular salary and benefits may be another, both now and in the future. Twenty years ago contingent workers, largely clerical, comprised one-quarter of the work force. By the year 2000, the number of temporary workers will double! And, they won't be limited to clerical or secretarial jobs; in fact, today, architects, nurses, paralegals, accountants, financial analysts, senior managers — even former CEO troubleshooters with high-level management experience — now work as subcontractors, often not by choice but because of necessity.

Borrowing on the just-in-time principle of inventory management, businesses throughout the country have downsized, or "right-sized," their work force. The epoch of just-in-time (JIT, as it is known in management circles) is here to stay. Stan Paz, superintendent in El Paso, Texas, is well aware his students feel there won't be enough jobs once they graduate. "Schools must change their focus to prepare students for the changing economic reality," he cautions. Michael Ward, superintendent, Oxford, North Carolina, adds, "Students have been made graphically aware of

Pamela Hatcher, a single mother of two, managed to hold onto her job with the D.C. government —
no small feat in a time of fiscal crisis and budget cutting. Her eldest, Joy, won a $72,000, four-year scholarship to the University of Pennsylvania. And her youngest daughter, Kelly, was accepted to Banneker, the city's academically rigorous high school.
The Hatcher girls' story is a living example of the oft-quoted African proverb that it takes an entire village to raise a child. Hatcher credits their triumphs to the support she has gotten over the years from her parents, friends, and church...."Everything is going well for us," Hatcher said. "But you worry from day to day that something will happen and it will all fall apart."

—Sari Horwitz,
"A Mother's Rewards,"
The Washington Post,
December 29, 1994,
p. D.C. 1-2

"Youth are rightfully fearful and bewildered at the severe narrowing of career, vocational, and economic prospects, and of opportunities to learn useful, productive, and rewarding skills."

—Bernard Z. Friedlander, Ph.D.,
Department of Psychology,
University of Hartford,
Hartford, Connecticut

both the perceived shortcomings of American public education and of their own need to be competitive in a rapidly changing world economy."

So great is the pressure, some students give up and drop out. Yet, says Kenna Seal, superintendent, Sutton, West Virginia, other students and parents view education as the key to empowerment and economic success and security.

Given the scarcity of jobs, the changing needs of the marketplace, and the technology explosion in the work place, it is imperative schools graduate students who are of value to future employers, which means much more than skill training. Today's and tomorrow's businesses will require people with flexibility, tolerance of failure, esprit de corps, a driving passion for excellence, cross-disciplinary capability, an understanding of different cultures, and a desire to serve the customer. And schools need the support of business in teaching such skills. "If a businessperson does not value a high school diploma, neither will the kids," says Joan Kowal, superintendent, Volusia County, Florida.

Part Three:

Prescriptives From Our Leading Educators

Now that we've examined the sociocultural context for the changes our leading educators cited among today's students, we turn to educators' recommendations for addressing the problems and challenges facing today's students, parents, and communities.

Given that students today have changed, that they've become disenfranchised, only a concerted collaborative

"Certainly, I've seen many changes [among students]. But, children remain the same: loving, open, and hungry to talk and to be listened to. Today's stressful and hurried world offers very little time for that. With all the pressures of 'performance,' standards, outcomes, basics, technology, etc., it seems sometimes giving a child 5-10 minutes of complete and unplanned attention is next to impossible. And yet, when I go into classrooms or eat lunch with them every day, this is what makes their hearts soar! This one-on-one relationship and knowing that whatever they have to say is important to someone can make such a difference!"

—Pat Deck, M.A., school counselor, Adams County School District No. 1, Monterrey Elementary, Denver, Colorado

effort will make a difference. Communities and citizens must work to reestablish links between young people and become supportive, positive influences. All the superintendents AASA polled agreed schools must help parents, who are dealing with multiple pressures and time con-straints as never before. Kenneth Burnley, Superintendent, Colorado Springs, Colorado, and 1993 National Superintendent of the Year, says there must "be a partnership....When we do before-and-after school day care, we'll write a Request for Proposal, and bid it to the community...The community has to own this."

Likewise, superintendent Michael Ward, of Oxford, North Carolina, says collaboration works because parents become the schools' "stake-holders." When parents get involved, the net result is innovation, pride, and community support. Most important, students do better when their parents demonstrate they care. Ward enlists the support of government, community, and social agencies to provide non-educational services now expected from schools.

And, in Vancouver, Washington, Mayor Bruce Hagensen reports Superintendent James Parsley, Jr.'s partnerships with community organi-zations have made Vancouver's schools the "supporting framework of this community." Day care, health care, parenting classes, adult educa-tion, and clothing for needy students help ensure that students come to school ready to learn.

Needed: A Sense of Purpose

All students are at risk of succumbing to the constant bombardments of pressure and temptation of the media and from their peer group. To help students overcome their sense of futility and feelings of hopeless-ness — to revitalize the energy of our youth — counselors and educators must impart the sense that the future lies within each individual and help students acquire social competency, develop problem-solving skills, gain autonomy and control over decision-making, and develop a sense of purpose, says Carol A. Dahir, vice president supervisor/post-secondary, American School Counselor Association and Pupil Personnel Services Administrator, Nassau Board of Cooperative Education Services, Westbury, New York.

Collaborative empowerment. Bedford, Michigan, superintendent Herbert Moyer zeroes in on partnerships as part of a "Collaborative Empowerment" initiative focusing on parental responsibility. Through Moyer's Collaborative Empowerment program, parents now have a voice in school budget planning, curriculum development, textbook selection and teacher hiring.

Witness the results achieved by the 1995 Superintendent of the Year, Robert Spillane of Fairfax County, Virginia, where parental involvement is a high priority. Test scores are up; graduation rates are up; and dropout rates are down. As one parent put it, Spillane's award says "we have a very high reputation in the country, which is being recognized. It didn't come easily. It had to be fought for, and Dr. Spillane has led the fight. We've stood shoulder to shoulder with him as a parent organization."

Keep the Home Fires Burning

A Reader's Digest/Louis Harris survey in 1994 of 2,130 high school students showed a high correlation between family and success in school. Happy homes resulted in confident kids who believed they could make things better for themselves and others.

"Parents, not schools, remain the most important educators of children. Create a sense of learning within the home itself,"[24] says former U.S. Secretary of Education, Lauro F. Cavazos, who suggests that parents should limit TV watching and fill their home with books and other educational materials.

While it is our schools' responsibility to educate and to inspire our young, they cannot — nor should they have to — shoulder the responsibility of parenting. Parents must help young people turn their despair and anger into hope.

As Candace Childress, a senior at Washington, D.C.'s Wilson High School put it, "Where would your generation be without parents who were there for you, helping with homework? With parents there for us, we know we can succeed." [25]

> *"School counselors must be the caring connection to strengthen the ties between the school, the family, and the community."*
>
> —Carol A. Dahir,
> vice president supervisor/
> Post-secondary,
> American School
> Counselor Association and
> pupil personnel services
> administrator,
> Nassau Board of
> Cooperative
> Education Services,
> Westbury, New York

Community Connections and Commitment

Business and media executives should examine their moral responsibility to support educators and weigh the consequences of selling products that glamorize violence. Be it donating computer equipment, giving parents time off to be with their children and volunteer in the community, hiring student interns, or giving classes at local schools, there are other tangible ways the business community can demonstrate their commitment to our children's future. Religious and community leaders, too, face a great challenge, particularly in this budget-cutting era, to help provide services for children in need. (See Figure 6, p. 38.)

---

24 "Secrets of Learning," *Family Circle*, September 4, 1990, p.86.
25 Courtland Milloy, "Parents Due for a Lesson," Metro, *The Washington Post,* February 5, 1995, p. B1.

Helping Children Become "Media Literate": Seven Tips for TV Viewing in the Home

The Center for Media Literacy, headquartered in Los Angeles, offers these ideas for helping to make television viewing a positive family experience:

1. Establish limits on how much TV your family watches. Decide the number of hours to watch each week and stick to it!

2. Plan your TV viewing. Encourage a family attitude that television should be turned on only to watch a specific show, not just to "see what's on." Choose your shows ahead of time, using a weekly television program guide.

3. Develop family guidelines for selecting programs. Be sure to discuss values you believe are important and the reasons for your choices. Check channel listings, including cable, and note reviews of programs with themes and subjects that match your family guidelines. Look for shows and videos that offer different viewpoints and help in your child's education.

4. Make TV watching an interactive family event. Television doesn't have to end family discussion and interaction. Watch it together, and use every opportunity to talk about what you are seeing and hearing. Use story lines or characters to stimulate conversation on topics that can be difficult to discuss: family relationships, feelings, appropriate sexual behavior, divorce or death. Try "thinking out loud" as a non-threatening way to let your children hear your values and prompt their response.

5. Talk back to your TV. When appropriate, express your opinions by "talking" directly to the TV as you watch. Respond to sexism, racism, and unnecessary violence, but point out positive portrayals as well. Don't forget to challenge commercials and the way they try to sell us not only products, but attitudes and lifestyles.

6. Let TV expand and enlarge your world. Find related books and magazine articles at your public library, and go on family outings based on ideas you've seen on TV. Keep an atlas or globe next to your television and find places mentioned in the news.

7. Be positive about TV's contribution to our world. Television is the dominant force in our media culture and an important part of children's lives. It should be evaluated fairly, not denigrated.

—The Center for Media Literacy is creating a broader view of literacy by helping people understand, analyze, and evaluate the media. The Center believes media literacy education is the sensible alternative to censorship.

Conclusion

Given the stresses of modern times and the breadth and rate of change in our society, many of us have chosen to insulate ourselves against the problems of youth. However, we must ask ourselves if we as a people have unknowingly or inadvertently abrogated our responsibility to instill in our children the values of decency, honesty, fairness, honor, duty, work, respect for others, courage, tolerance, and responsibility for one's actions. We must examine how our actions and behavior, how our time away from our children affects our children. Don't we — not only parents, but all of us — owe them more?

Today, more than ever, social passivity is not an acceptable or viable solution. If, as so many in our society believe, we are searching for meaning in our lives, what greater purpose do we have in our lives than our children?

Many parents, schools, and communities across the country have chosen to view the problems of our youth as challenges and opportunities for change. They've moved beyond blame and indifference to involvement. From individual to community solutions. From despair to dreams.

The purpose of this booklet is to encourage you — educators and counselors; business and media executives; religious, government, and community leaders; and parents most especially — to become part of the solution. Whether or not you have children, the stakes of ignoring the nation's children are high. Our character as a nation, the democratic principles we hold true and dear, our ability to compete in the global economy, our capacity to innovate, our financial health, the quality of life in communities, the safety and rights of our citizens, and our most precious institution, the family — all are at stake.

It's time to join a "crusade" for our children. All of us have a moral imperative to shepherd our children. If we want our children to become responsible citizens, we must act accordingly.

Figure 6: A Vision of Communities Where Learning Can Happen

Source: U.S. Department of Education and U.S. Department of Health and Human Services, Together We Can, *Atelia I. Melaville, Center for the Study of Social Policy; and Martin J. Blank, Institute for Educational Leadership, with Gelareh Asayesh, April 1993.*

Acknowledgments

I n addition to Superintendents of the Year, the following people and sources have been a source of inspiration to this booklet.

A special thanks to Dr. Morris Massey, Morris Massey Associates, Boulder, Colorado, and former Associate Dean of Undergraduate Studies, University of Colorado College of Business, Boulder, Colorado, who helped pinpoint the sociocultural trends and significant events that shaped each generation's values, attitudes, beliefs, and lifestyles.

The author and AASA are grateful for guidance provided by Dr. Thomas C. Barrett, child psychologist and author; Dr. Gerald W. Bracey, policy analyst, education researcher, and author; Marvin Cetron, forecaster, Forecasting International, Arlington, Virginia; Carol A. Dahir, pupil personnel services administrator, Nassau Board of Cooperative Education Services, Westbury, New York, and vice president, American School Counselor Association; Pam Deck, M.A., counselor, Adams County School District No. 1, Denver, Colorado; Dr. Harold L. Hodgkinson, author and demographer, Institute for Educational Leadership, Washington, D.C.; Dr. Paul Houston, executive director, American Association of School Administrators, Arlington, Virginia; Pat Lane, American Association of School Administrators, Arlington, Virginia; Captain Vince McInerney, commander, Media Relations Office, Kansas City, Missouri Police Department, Kansas City, Missouri; Barbara Johnson, counselor, Bertha Reid Elementary School, Thornton, Colorado; Nancy Rochur, senior professional associate, Communications, National Education Association, Washington, D.C.; Tony Silva, public relations specialist, Whitman-Walker Clinic, Inc., Washington, D.C.; Dr. Elwood L. Shafer, Fulbright research scholar and professor, environmental management, Department of Health and Human Development, School of Hotel, Restaurant and Institutional Management, The Pennsylvania State University, University Park, Pennsylvania; Carolyn S. Shaffer, Ph.D., Center for Cognitive Therapy, Bethesda, Maryland; Diane Shewmaker, counselor, Owen Valley Middle School, Spencer, Indiana, and President, Indiana School Counselor Association; U.S. Senator Paul Simon's office; Bonnie Smith, teacher, Hettinger Public School, Hettinger, North Dakota, and 1994 North Dakota, Teacher of the Year; Dr. Kathleen Smith, clinical psychologist, The Family Therapy Institute, Alexandria, Virginia; and Bernard Z. Friedlander, professor, Department of Psychology, University of Hartford, Hartford, Connecticut.

The information by the following organizations and books was of tremendous value as well.

Advocates for Youth (formerly, The Center for Population Control); American Federation of Teachers; American School Counselor Association; Association for Educational Communications & Technology; Association for Supervision and Curriculum Development; William Bennett, The Book of Virtues; Allan Bloom, The Closing of the American Mind; The Center for Substance Abuse Prevention, National Clearinghouse for Alcohol and Drug Information; Children's Defense Fund; Council of Chief State School Officers; Educational Communications, Inc.; Education Research Service; Greater Washington Boys & Girls Clubs; Handgun Control, Inc.; Institute for Educational Leadership; International Technology Education Association; Richard Mitchell, The Graves of Academe; National Aids Clearinghouse; National Congress of Parents and Teachers; National Council for Year-Round Education; National Crime Prevention Council; National Education Association; Operation Understanding, New York; "The Popcorn Report," Faith Popcorn; U.S. Department of Education; U.S. Department of Health and Human Services, National Institute of Drug Abuse and National Institute of Mental Health; U.S. and Department of Justice.

The author also thanks participants in the many education forums on the internet and the fine work some of our leading journalists are doing on all of our behalf: "Teen Empowerment," Eye on America, CBS Evening News; Bill Moyer's series, "What We Can Do About Violence" and "Frontline" (PBS); Charlayne Hunter-Gault's series on violence, "The MacNeil/Lehrer News Hour" (PBS); "Inside The Law," (WHMM), Baltimore, Maryland; "Roots of Crime," (WJLA), Washington, D.C.

Former USA Today Education Editor Pat Ordovensky wrote the original manuscript. Publications Manager Leslie Eckard and Natalie Carter Holmes, editor of Leadership News, edited subsequent drafts and supervised production, with assistance from Patrick McHugh. AASA Sr. Associate Executive Director Gary Marx served as project director. Darlene Pierce, director of the Superintendent of the Year program, was instrumental in helping to identify sources and gather information. Graphic Design was provided by Lea Croteau Bartlett of East Woods Studio in Sherwood Forest, Maryland.